HANDLING
DISRESPECT
10 useful stoic
lessons for
handling disrespect
ADRIAN WALTERS

Table Of Contents

Introduction

We all encounter disrespect in various aspects in life. The way we react during such occasions determines the level at which the disrespect received will affect our lives in general. When we take disrespect to heart, we tend to react rather rashly to it thereby affecting our future in ways that are uncertain. On the other hand when we see disrespect as a normal occurrence in life, we make use of the most peaceful approach to correct and curb it, thereby opening ways to new and better relationships for us.

This book outlines and explains 10 stoic principles that can guide us in handling disrespect gracefully.

Lesson One

Maintain Inner Peace

Stoics often refer to Epictetus who said that, "People are disturbed not by things, but by the view they take of them." This quote underscores that our reactions are based on our interpretations not the events themselves. Stoics emphasized that our emotional responses are not determined by external events but by our interpretations of those events.

Disrespect for instance is not inherently upsetting. It is our perception and judgment of it that cause distress. When someone disrespects you, it is crucial to recognize that their behavior is a reflection of their own thoughts, feelings and judgments, rather than an objective assessment of your worth. This understanding can help you maintain your inner peace by not allowing their disrespect to disturb your emotional equilibrium.

Lesson Two

Practice Self-reflection

Marcus Aurelius reminds us to look inward. The happiness in your life depends upon the quality of your thoughts. Stoicism encourages individuals to engage in introspection and self-examination. The stoics believed that a key aspect of wisdom and self-improvement is thenability to reflect on one's thoughts and behaviors.

When you encounter disrespect, it is essential to engage in self-reflection. Ask yourself questions like; is there any truth in what the person said or did? Did my own actions or words contribute to this situation? How can I respond in a way that aligns with my values and virtues? By examining your reactions and the situation objectively, you can gain a better understanding of the event and your own role in it. This introspection allows you to respond more thoughtfully and constructively to disrespect.

In summary, practicing self-reflection in the face of disrespect is a stoic way to ensure that your responses are based on rational judgment rather than impulsive reactions. It helps you learn from the situation and promotes personal growth and wisdom.

Lesson Three

Don't React Impulsively

Seneca advises that whenever you are angry be assured that it is not only a present evil but that you have increased a habit. Stoics believe in the importance of self-control and rationality. They argue that impulsive reactions driven by intense emotions like anger or frustration often lead to poor decisions and unnecessary suffering.

When faced with disrespect, the stoic approach encourages you to avoid reacting impulsively. Instead, take a moment to pause and collect your thoughts. This pause allows you to regain control over your emotions and gives you the opportunity to respond in a more measured and thoughtful manner. By resisting the impulse to react immediately, you can better align your response with stoic principles of wisdom and self-control. This approach often leads to more constructive and less emotionally charged interactions when faced with disrespect.

In summary, not reacting impulsively is a key stoic strategy tobmaintain composure and make rational decisions when confronted with disrespect, ultimately leading to more positive outcomes and personal growth.

Lesson Four

Empathy

Stoics advocate understanding the other person's perspective. As Epictetus put it, "seek not the good in external things, seek it in yourselves." Stoics believe in the interconnectedness of humanity and that understanding the motivations and emotions of others can lead to better interactions and personal growth. When someone shows disrespect stoicism suggests practicing empathy. Try to put yourself in the other person's shoes and understand their perspective. Consider factors such as their background experiences and current emotional state. By empathizing with the person who is disrespectful you can gain insight into why they might be behaving this way. Avoid reacting defensively or aggressively. Respond with patience and understanding rather than anger.

Practicing empathy when faced with disrespect aligns with stoic values of wisdom, compassion and self-improvement. It allows you to respond to challenging situations with a more balanced and compassionate mindset, fostering better relationships and personal development.

Lesson Five

Focus On Virtue

A core stoic principle is cultivating virtues like wisdom and courage. Seneca advises virtue is nothing else than right reason. Stoicism places a significant emphasis on the pursuit of virtue as the highest good in life. Virtues are qualities of character that lead to a life of excellence and fulfillment.

According to stoic philosophy, when encountering disrespect stoicism suggests focusing on virtue in your response. This means considering how you canbrespond in a way that aligns with your stoic values and virtue. By focusing on virtue when confronted with disrespect, stoicism encourages you to respond in a way that upholds your moral principles, maintains your integrity and contributes to personal growth. It's about striving to be the best version of yourself even in challenging situation.

Lesson Six

Acceptance

Stoicism teaches us to accept that disrespect is a part of life. As Epictetus said, "He is a wise man who does not grieve for the things which he is not, but rejoices for those which he has." Stoicism teaches that we should focus our efforts and concerns on things that are within our control known as the stoic dichotomy of control.

External events including the behavior of others, are often beyond our control therefore acceptance becomes a vital aspect of maintaining inner peace. When you encounter disrespect, stoicism suggests accepting the reality that disrespect is a common experience in life. It's not something you can entirely prevent or change as you have no control over the actions and attitudes of others.

Lesson Seven

Humor

Sometimes humor can be a powerful tool. As Seneca noted, you become a master of yourself when you learn how to handle where you should not carry the mask of tragedy. While stoicism emphasizes self-control and rational responses, it also acknowledges the power of humor in managing difficult situations. Humor can be a means of maintaining emotional balance and avoiding excessive anger or irritation. When confronted with disrespect, using humor can be a stoic strategy to respond effectively instead of reacting with anger or defensiveness. You can choose to respond in a way that injects levity into the situation.

While humor should be used judiciously, in an appropriate situations, it can be a valuable stoic tool for responding to disrespect in a way that promotes a more positive and harmonious outcome.

Lesson Eight

Set Boundaries

Stoicism teaches the importance of maintaining one's dignity and self-respect. While stoic's focus on inner control, they also recognize that it's within their control to establish and communicate appropriate boundary. When confronted with disrespect, stoicism suggests that you should calmly and assertively communicate your boundaries to the person displaying disrespect. This involves letting them know what behavior is unacceptable to you and what you expect in terms of respectful treatment.

Setting boundaries aligns with stoic values of self-respect justice and courage. It allows you to protect your well-being, maintain your integrity and ensure that you're not subjected to ongoing disrespect. Stoicism doesn't advocate passive acceptance of mistreatment, but encourages a proactive approach to maintaining one's dignity and self-control in challenging situation.

Lesson Nine

Forgiveness

Stoics Advocate forgiveness, not for the other person's benefit but for your own peace of mind. Seneca wisely said, "To forgive all is as inhuman as to forgive none." Stoicism emphasizes the importance of inner tranquility and living in accordance with virtue.

Forgiveness is seen as a means to achieve this tranquility as holding onbto negative emotions can be detrimentalbto one's own mental and emotional health. When someone disrespects you, stoicism suggests considering the option of forgiveness. This doesn't mean condoning or excusing the disrespectful behavior, but rather letting go of the negative emotions associated with it. Forgiveness and stoicism involved recognizing that holding on to anger or resentment harms you more than the person who disrespected you, choosing to release these negative emotions as an act of self-compassion and personal growth, focusing on moving forward with a sense of inner peace and tranquility.

In essence, forgiveness in stoicism is a way to prioritize your own mental and emotional well-being over holding onto grudges. It aligns with the stoic principle of focusing on what's within your control and letting go of what isn't. By forgiving, you free yourself from the burden of anger and resentment allowing you to maintain inner peace and moveforward with a more positive outlook.

Lesson Ten

Perspective: Consider The Bigger Picture

In the grand scheme of life, most instances of disrespect are minor. As Marcus Aurelius reminds us our, life is what our thoughts make. Stoicism encourages individuals to cultivate a rational and balanced view of life's challenges. Disrespect is seen as one of thesenchallenges and adopting the rightbperspective can help maintain inner tranquility. When confronted with disrespect, stoicism suggests that you should consider the bigger picture. Recognize that most instances of disrespect are relatively minor and temporary in the context of your entire life. Applying perspective involves avoiding the exaggeration of the importance of the disrespect in the long term, refraining from dwelling on the incident, excess focusing on your goals, values and what truly matters in life rather than fixating on the disrespectful behavior. In essence, adopting perspective in stoicism helps you keep a level head when faced with disrespect. It allows you to maintain your emotional balance by recognizing that most instances of disrespect are fleeting and should not have a long lasting negative impact on your well-being. By keeping the bigger picture in mind, you can navigate such situations with equanimity and wisdom.

Conclusion

So there you have it, a stoic guide on how to deal with disrespect. Remember stoicism isn't about suppressing emotions but channeling them wisely. By applying these principles you can maintain your inner peace and resilience in the face of disrespect.